CHIMPANZEES

MONKEY DISCOVERY LIBRARY

Lynn M. Stone

Rourke Corporation, Inc.
Vero Beach, Florida 32964

PHOTO CREDITS

All photos © Lynn M. Stone

ACKNOWLEDGEMENTS

The author thanks the following for photographic assistance:
Chester Zoo, Chester, England; Lowry Park Zoological Garden,
Tampa, Fla.; Miami Metrozoo, Fla.

LIBRARY OF CONGRESS
Library of Congress Cataloging-in-Publication Data
Stone, Lynn M.
  Chimpanzees / by Lynn M. Stone.

  p. cm. — (Monkey discovery library)
  Summary: An introduction tothe playful, outgoing champanzee.
  ISBN 0-86593-064-3
  1. Champanzee—Juvenile literature. [1. Chimpanzee.]
I. Title. II. Series: Stone, Lynn M. Monkey discovery library.
QL737.P96S77   1990
599.88'44—dc20   90-32422
                                   CIP
                                   AC

Printed in the USA

TABLE OF CONTENTS

THE CHIMPANZEE

Like some people you may know, chimpanzees love to show off. People who watch chimpanzees chatter and rush about often see actions that remind them of themselves, too!

Playful chimps are in many ways like people. They can stand upright and grasp objects with their hands. They have large brains, and they can make simple tools. They have flat faces and eyes which look forward.

There are two kinds, or **species,** of chimpanzee. The common chimpanzee *(Pan troglodytes)* is larger than the bonobo or pygmy chimp *(Pan paniscus).*

THE CHIMPANZEE'S COUSINS

The chimpanzees' closest relatives are the gorilla and orangutan. Together with the gorilla and orang, chimpanzees are great apes, or super-sized monkeys.

The apes and monkeys belong to a group of intelligent mamals called primates. Humans are also primates.

Monkeys and apes are much different from people. Still, the great apes especially have many things in common with people.

Orangutan

HOW THEY LOOK

Chimpanzees are furry and generally black with a white patch near their rump. A chimp's face is usually bare. Its nose, hands, feet, and ears are the color of light flesh.

Chimps have a ridge of bone along their foreheads. Like the other great apes, they have no tail.

Common chimpanzees stand up to five feet and weigh 95 to 120 pounds. Pygmy chimps are shorter and weigh 55 to 100 pounds.

WHERE THEY LIVE

Chimpanzees live only in western and central Africa. Most of them live in warm, rainy forests. Others live in low forests that are not as dense or wet.

Some chimps have an altogether different kind of home, or **habitat.** They live in mountain forests up 9,000 feet above the level of the sea.

Chimpanzees stay away from mountain forests where their mountain gorilla cousins live.

The pygmy chimp lives in swampy forests in central Zaire (pronounced zi-EAR).

Chimpanzee

Sleeping chimp

HOW THEY LIVE

Chimps are fond of each other's company. They live in groups, or **troops,** of 30 to 80 animals.

Chimps often hug and **groom** each other. Chimps groom by combing fur with their long fingers. Grooming helps remove dirt and insects.

Chimps are fine climbers. Sometimes they swing from tree to tree. More often, however, they travel on the ground by walking or running on all fours.

Chimps are active and noisy. They can be very fierce toward each other.

Chimpanzee troop

THE CHIMPANZEE'S BABIES

A baby chimp weighs about four pounds at birth. When mom travels, the baby hangs onto its mother's underside. At six months, the baby chimp "moves upstairs" and rides on mom's back.

Like people and other great apes, chimps grow up slowly. A young chimp stays with its mother up to eight years. It does not become an adult until it reaches its teens.

Chimps live to be perhaps 60 years old in the wild.

PREDATOR AND PREY

Chimpanzees eat both plant and animal foods. Most of their food is fruit, flowers, and other plant parts.

Sometimes chimpanzees are hunting animals, or **predators.** They hunt and kill young monkeys and bush pigs. These animals are their **prey.**

Chimps like insects, too. They have learned to poke a stick into a termite nest. The insects climb onto the stick. The chimp pulls the stick out and snacks on the termites.

Very few animals have learned to use tools.

himpanzee

THE CHIMPANZEE AND PEOPLE

People have studied chimpanzees for many years. Chimps have been used for the study of human diseases.

To help solve space flight problems, a chimp was once sent into space on a U.S. rocket.

In 1972, Jane Goodall, a scientist, began studying wild chimpanzees. Her work has helped us learn how intelligent chimpanzees are. Captive chimps have been taught to use sign language.

THE CHIMPANZEE'S FUTURE

Chimps in parks, such as Gombe National Park, are usually quite safe. Chimpanzees which are not protected in parks are always in danger. Their forest homes are being destroyed.

African forests are used for wood and to make room for farms.

Hunters are also a danger. Chimps are shot for food and because they sometimes raid farms for fruits and vegetables.

Chimpanzees are one of our smartest animals. But they cannot survive without man's help.

Glossary

groom (GROOM)—to comb and clean fur by using the fingers

habitat (HAB a tat)—the kind of place in which an animal lives, such as rain forest

predator (PRED a tor)—an animal that kills other animals for food

prey (PRAY)—an animal that is hunted by another for food

species (SPEE sheez)—within a group of closely related animals, one certain kind

troop (TROOP)—a group of monkeys or apes

INDEX